YOUR DOG'S STAR SIGN

REVEALED BY
JILL INGLIS

FLEETFOOT BOOKS

First published in the United Kingdom
and Continental Europe 1994 by .
Fleetfoot Books
    a division of Gazelle Book Services Limited,
Falcon House,
Queen Square,
Lancaster LA1 1RN
England

ISBN 1 85586 0074

Edited by Sarah Brenan
Illustrated by Tony Irving
Typeset by Butler Graphics Pty Ltd, Richmond, Victoria 3121
Produced by Island Graphics Pty Ltd
Printed in Singapore

ACKNOWLEDGEMENTS

I am deeply indebted to Kerry Cussen for guiding me along the right path, and at the same time providing the motivation that I sometimes lacked. I would also like to thank Maria Prendergast for giving me the benefit of her expertise and experience in the field of writing.

Thanks to Lisa Johnson, Margot Casey and Laura Rowles for their help and comments, and special thanks to my dogs for their inspiration and friendship.

FOR MY MOTHER, PAT EVANS

INTRODUCTION

Dogs have been closely linked with man since time immemorial, and most people, at some stage of their lives, have enjoyed the love and companionship that a dog provides.

A dog's loyalty is his* most treasured quality, and one which binds him to his owner for life; but some are more loyal than others, and personality and behaviour vary with each individual animal. The aim of this book is to outline the basic canine characteristics relevant to each of the twelve signs of the zodiac. To pinpoint the beginning and end of an astrological sign, I chose to use the dates supplied by Cheiro in his book *When Were You Born?* They differ slightly from those used by most astrologers, as he states that the twenty-first day of each month signifies the commencement of a new sign, and then further explains 'that for seven days it is overlapped by the cusp of the previous sign, and does not come into its full power until on, or about, the 28th day'. In other words, those born in the cusp will take from the qualities of both signs. I am of the opinion that dog lovers who are anxious to identify their canines with an astrological sign will find this system easier. If the date of your pet's birth can only be guessed at, it is worth exploring the text to find a section (or a combination of two) that best sums up his personality.

* *I have used the masculine pronoun in the Introduction but alternated 'he'/'she' in the text; but of course any of my comments could apply equally to the other gender.*

5

Because man is considered a highly complex being, both in thought and deed, certain aspects of human behaviour are not readily applicable to dogs, for our pets have a far more simplistic view of life. To adapt astrological descriptions intended for humans proved to be a formidable task, and I interviewed numerous dog owners in my search for accuracy. Like their human counterparts, dogs have some foibles, and each sign in the zodiac is shown to produce its share of strengths and weaknesses. For example, I have described the Arian dog as one not given to humility or modesty, but he is capable of loving without question.

Numerous tales have been told of the psychic abilities possessed by animals, and it is possible dogs have experienced many lives. In the chapter dealing with the Piscean pet, you will discover that he is an especially intuitive and mystical creature. Pisces is a combination of all the signs that precede it, and symbolises the end of the circle, so many astrologers link it to the spirit world.

I have avoided dealing with any of the technical aspects of astrology, as my knowledge in this field is very limited. There are a number of excellent books available for those readers wishing to undertake further study; as well as Cheiro's *When Were You Born?* my research included Linda Goodman's *Sun Signs* and Joanna Martine Woolfolk's *The Only Astrology Book You'll Ever Need*. Most astrologers agree that Aries signifies a new beginning, the start of the circle of life, and this is why I begin the book with that sign.

Finally, a note on canine cuisine — I have given a recipe for each star sign, and most of these have been carefully selected for their nutritional value. Family and friends were persuaded to pass on invaluable kennel lore, for wise dog owners know that many a pooch can appear to be pedigreed if correctly conditioned. The selection of recipes is not large, but interesting in its content. Some of the cooking involved requires ingredients that will test the fortitude of even the most dedicated cook,

6

but the addition of herbs to the pot and sufficient ventilation in the kitchen can help to reduce unpleasant odours. Meat, either raw or cooked, should appear on the menu whenever possible, but both canned and dried food provide a nutritionally complete meal. To avoid a build-up of calculus on your pet's teeth, it is advisable to provide bones for him to chew upon. Access to fresh water is essential, and some dogs are a lot thirstier than others.

I hope you find a certain humour in these pages, as well as gaining a deeper insight into the mind of your dog.

Jill Inglis

ARIES

The zodiacal sign of Aries commences on 21 March, but does not come into its full power until about 27 March.

The dog born during this period is aware only of herself, tending to put her own needs above all others. She is an unusually friendly animal with a positive, forceful manner, so much so that people are inclined to reach out and pat her as she passes them in the street. Your Aries pet feels instinctively that her needs should come first, and as the household has to be the pivot of her world, naturally she manages to learn how to control it from an early age. She somehow achieves this without resorting to devious or cunning behaviour — these traits are unlikely to be found in an Arian. An air of innocence, coupled with a somewhat naive outlook on life, softens a personality that otherwise might be deemed abrasive.

The Aries dog seems unable to learn that experience is the best teacher, so it can be puzzling to watch her repeat an action that maybe yesterday, or the day before, spelled disaster. With most Aries pets, there appears to be an inability to accept the fact that life can be full of pain and danger; caution is an unknown word in their vocabulary.

Unfortunately the Arian canine's lack of fear overcomes logic. When commonsense is disregarded she can easily find herself in hazardous situations, her lack of traffic sense being a prime example, and she is inclined to suddenly leap across the road if something catches her attention on the other side.

8

With an Aries dog there is a tendency to act aggressively towards other animals — she is a born fighter and very brave when facing larger opponents. Fearless though she is, physical pain is something her system cannot tolerate. Once she is aware of pain this dog becomes very vocal, and one is inclined to think the worst, but more often than not the injury is minor. Still, she is never hesitant about engaging in combat, fighting without thought for the damage that might be inflicted upon her person, or the pain it is going to cause.

This canine's love of her own voice can create problems at home, as it would never enter her head that she might be behaving selfishly and keeping not only her household awake, but the neighbours as well. Often the reasons for this behaviour are unclear; maybe she is trying to prove that she does most things better than anyone else.

A dog born under this sign is always in a great hurry, and though not a graceful animal, nevertheless holds her tail at a jaunty angle and generally carries herself well. She is not the nervous, twitchy type — so it would be unusual to encounter a neurotic Arian. The egotistical nature possessed by this pet has no room for a humble or patient attitude, humility and modesty are rarely learnt, except after many dismal experiences. Puppy habits are retained throughout a large part of the dog's life, therefore the owner can expect to find holes dug in the garden, and belongings occasionally mangled. The Arian is not an entirely responsible watchdog, but when least expected, shows her prowess at minding the home and children in a most efficient, businesslike way.

The sign of Aries the Ram represents the element of fire, so you can expect your pet to have sudden flare-ups and exhibit temperamental behaviour. As she rarely bears a grudge, the fire tends to subside just as quickly as it was lit. Brief though these outbursts are, she is not always a suitable pet for very young children, unless they are taught never to take liberties to the extreme.

a born fighter . . . very prone to cuts about the head

If one can overlook these slight flaws in the Arian's temperament, she is an ideal dog to own, given her uncomplicated nature and an ability to love and trust without question.

Your Aries pet is very prone to cuts about the head, usually received during the course of a fight, so this is the area you will most likely be treating more frequently than others. The animal's eyesight might be poor — in later life blindness is a problem — but again, because of her courageous nature, the Aries dog is able to adapt well to such a disability. She is susceptible to chills, and it is important to dry her off after she has been exposed to wet weather for any length of time. Some dogs born during this period may be plagued by skin rashes, and suffer from stomach disorders during the hot weather, but seldom does this canine fall victim to chronic diseases. Aries seems to produce a far greater percentage of stroke victims and acute illnesses than lingering disorders.

An Arian dog is rarely gloomy, and is blessed with a positive attitude that overcomes adversity. The animal pushes ahead with confidence, at times oblivious to the feelings of others. Remember, she just believes in herself. Your dog, if allowed on the street, does not waste time hanging about with other canines in idle talk, but is more inclined to muster them together and head for parts unknown. She is a natural leader and others recognise this gift immediately, following her without question.

The Arian dog is always in search of something new to discover, so she can roam for miles without seeming to tire. It is obviously preferable to try and confine her to home boundaries, especially as the pet exudes friendliness. She is inclined to approach strangers without taking heed of the consequences, so is likely to become an easy target for the ranger; thus entailing a stay in the dog pound, and causing her owner unnecessary expense and embarrassment.

The owner of an Arian must try to tone down the pet's brashness, as the animal has to be made continually aware of the fact that there are others in life who need to be considered. You might notice her desire for attention becomes more apparent when you are speaking on the telephone, entertaining friends, or otherwise engaged. It is not that this dog is jealous; quite the contrary, she just wants affirmation as to her position of number one!

The Aries pet can frequently act on impulse, so therefore lacks caution exploring new territories, and as we have seen, has little regard for any of the associated dangers. You would be well advised to bring her to heel by providing a suitable diversion, rather than constantly reprimanding an animal who revels in the excitement provided by her daily existence.

An Aries personality exudes a strength that makes other canines look pale in comparison, and few can keep up with the boundless energy and optimism of the Arian. The puppy born during this period is very strong, hard to house-train, and accident-prone. The animal has a deep-seated fear of being unloved and rejected, as demonstrated by occasional outbursts of overwhelming affection towards all and sundry. This pet frets if chained up, and can create noise in the most alarming way when confined against her will.

The Aries dog finds the most harmony in her life comes from being in an environment where all shades of red, crimson, rose and pink are likely to be featured. During illness she may show a preference for blue and violet, as these colours seem to have a healing effect upon the pet.

Arian canines find more lasting friendships with those born in their own period, and those born under the signs of Leo, Sagittarius and Scorpio.

Fang Cake

This is an adaptable recipe, as various fillings can be used. An Arian canine is always prepared to try something new — it is unusual to find a finicky eater amongst Aries pets. Greed often overcomes the need for niceties at mealtimes, and your dog can make a terrible mess of the ingredients on her plate. Everything is normally eaten in record time, and the dish licked clean.

The dog born under the sign of the Ram literally radiates good health for most if not all of her life, and often goes to any lengths to procure food. She becomes adept at raiding rubbish tins for the sake of an extra titbit. This recipe should please her, and fulfil all her dietary needs.

A variation on the classical pancake, this recipe contains rice.

2 eggs   *2 tablespoons flour*
1 cup cooked rice   *1 cup milk*

Slightly beat the eggs, sift in flour, then add the rice and milk. Stir well before pouring into a well oiled frying pan. Cook gently, and keep turning sections of the pancake until it is light brown in colour. This makes a good breakfast dish for a hungry hound, but if you choose to serve it as an evening meal remember to include a filling of your own creation. Interesting fillings can be made from chopped meat, either raw or cooked; chicken, grated carrot and a small amount of grated cheese is another option.

TAURUS

THE BULL

The zodiacal sign of Taurus commences on 20 April, but does not come into its full power until on or about 27 April.

Dogs born in this section of the year have the ability to dominate everything and everyone about them without even being conscious of trying to do so. As a rule the Taurean canine is very determined, and can be completely unyielding is his attitude to those around him. For a large part of the day he prefers his own company, so it is wisest not to try and alter this routine, but leave him undisturbed.

A Taurus dog is considered by many to be the ideal pet for children. Because of his seemingly placid and stoical nature, he is capable of suffering all sorts of indignities. He is seldom cruel in his actions, but beware of the Taurus temper, though it is rarely displayed unless this pet has been pushed to the limits of his endurance. Nor does he give any warning of approaching danger, but when he charges there is a likelihood that all opponents will be demolished! It can take some time before the dust settles and the dog's routine goes back to normal; such rare outbursts of fury really upset him, disrupting his metabolism and desire for peace.

As the Taurean dog has such an obstinate nature, he is deaf to outside voices once he decides on a particular course of action. One is inclined to classify him as disobedient, but as he is normally such an honest animal he is not capable of being sly or underhand in his actions.

14

This dog is governed by a loving nature, being able to make great sacrifices for those he loves. As he is content with his own company so often, it is not necessary to provide another companion to keep him amused.

Observe sometimes your Taurean pet, cushioned in a blanket of flowers, gazing at the clear blue sky, and inhaling the perfumes of his garden. It is to be hoped that the majority of dogs born under the sign of the Bull can enjoy and experience this type of environment, for flowers play an integral part in their lives, and without them they can find that life becomes dull and grey.

Because the characteristics of the Taurus dog are so like those of the bull he represents, his own field is preferable to any other, and home is his castle. These pets tend to have an intangible bovine quality about them, enhanced by a slow-moving walk

gazing at the clear blue sky and inhaling the perfume of his garden

with a suggestion of great hidden strength. The Taurus canine is soothed by the browns and greens of nature, but the colours of the sky — all shades of blue, also rose and pink (to a lesser degree) — appeal to him most. One must be careful with red, as it can have a catalytic effect if displayed too prominently.

When handling the Taurus dog, it is better not to jolt him out of his complacency, but leave the day's decision-making to him. He will probably choose to stay at home rather than have an outing in the car, and is not going to waste energy, either by chasing the neighbouring cats, or finding other dogs in the street. He would rather receive visitors than make calls, preferring to follow a passive lifestyle.

The Taurean pet, whether large or small, is usually well-proportioned but with a tendency to obesity. His digestive system rarely fails him, and he can eat almost anything, but has a preference for beef above all other meats. He is not unduly fussy about the way in which his food is presented to him, but expects it to be served at the same time each day.

As the Taurus dog seldom worries or frets, neither is he the twitchy, nervous type. He rarely suffers from skin complaints or is bothered by fleas. If sick he is most stoical, putting on a very brave front — so much so that sometimes one does not realise that the complaint is quite serious.

This pet is exceptionally close to the earth, therefore he has a great love for the land, preferring a dry climate to the dampness and dullness associated with winter. If the dog is denied his share of fresh air, along with outdoor living, he tends to lose his superb health, over-eat, and then become obese. It is better to try and regulate his intake of food as much as possible, regardless of his unspoken appeals for more nourishment.

Obesity can put a great strain on the Taurean dog's heart, and back and leg troubles develop too, not to mention poor circulation, all factors which can shorten his life. These are problems that need not occur, and by good management they can be avoided. Regular exercise is essential for this pet, but will be more effective and beneficial if carried out at the same time each day, so as not to upset the tempo of his existence.

No dog can be kinder or more gentle than a Taurean; he is never cruel or vindictive, but an owner not in harmony with the pet will sometimes judge him unfairly. Because stubbornness and passivity can be very irritating, one can lose sight of the loyalty and devotion the Taurean dog has to offer. There is also a certain humour and earthiness within the Taurean spirit that if brought to the surface, nurtured and maintained can offset a great many other faults.

If a Taurean has to fight to defend his territory, he much prefers a large adversary to a smaller one, being impressed by all things large. A Taurus dog can fight to the death, and rarely retreats from battle. His rage, which we have observed as being violent but exceedingly rare, comes more readily to the surface when defending territory. This canine is not basically a trouble-seeker, so it is usually a stranger who initiates the trouble.

During a cold, wet spell, when your pet is unable to venture outside to lie among his favourite flowers, second best has to do. If a soft, furry blanket is used as a substitute, passive Taurus can while away the hours indoors, dreaming of sunny days to come.

Occasionally it will do no harm to activate him into taking a walk in the rain, if just to see some animation light upon his features.

Taurus finds the most lasting friendships are formed with dogs born under the Virgo, Libra, Scorpio and Capricorn signs.

Poodle Pizza

Your Taurus pet does not have to be a poodle to enjoy this dish, and whatever his breeding he will disregard the name in favour of the food. A satisfactory balance is obtained by the use of varied ingredients, and the beef-loving Taurus dog should be well satisfied after eating his pizza.

As the Taurean canine is inclined to obesity, it is wise to stand firm if he requests seconds, on the understanding that the recipe provides most of his daily dietary needs. If he appears to be really hungry, a good solid bone should suffice, for the dog born under the sign of the Bull is inclined to bolt down his food, and needs plenty of chewing time.

Poodle Pizza is guaranteed to make mealtime a momentous event, so I would suggest it appear on the menu whenever possible.

A chance conversation with a poodle owner led to the discovery of this very *chic* recipe. We both felt it should not be confined to an elite group. As you will see, it is simplicity itself.

1 piece stewing steak	*water*
(chopped)	*2 rashers bacon*
¾ cup rolled oats	*1 egg*

Slightly moisten rolled oats in a little water. Line an ovenproof dish with oats, then cover with beaten egg. Add meat and finally criss-cross with the bacon, which needs to be cut to size. Bake in a moderate oven for 30 minutes. Cool, and serve. Depending on the size of the piece of steak (and your dog!), this dish could suffice for two meals.

THE TWINS

GEMINI

The zodiacal sign of Gemini — the Twins — commences on 21 May, but does not come into its full power until on or about 28 May.

If your dog was born during this period she is certain to display two distinct sides to her personality. These twin sides of her nature tend to pull her in opposite directions, so she appears to lack continuity of purpose. The Gemini dog can run through a whole gamut of emotions in the time it takes to blink twice. No wonder you will sometimes despair of ever understanding her, and as she can blow hot and cold almost simultaneously, this will confuse you more. There is a restless quality about this pet, and she can act impulsively at the most inopportune moments. No matter how well-trained and disciplined she might appear to be, this facade can fall like a pack of cards when least expected. The Gemini pet is therefore inclined to disobey commands but it is better not to chastise her too severely as she is not always able to comprehend the reasons for her disrespectful behaviour.

If you wish to enjoy your pet's company, and seek her co-operation as much as possible, I would advise you to make her life as interesting and entertaining as your time allows. The Gemini dog has tremendous nervous energy to spare, and if confined to a small area will become an emotional wreck. At the best of times she finds it difficult to concentrate on one

19

object for more than a few seconds; so alert is she that her eyes constantly seek out something different to investigate.

Because your dog dislikes routine and cannot adapt to a monotonous existence, she is sometimes best suited to country life, away from the confinement and restrictions placed upon her in the city.

This animal is unusually quick on her feet, and prefers to run everywhere, providing she is not restricted by space. A Gemini pet is inclined to be a chronic wanderer, and if given the chance to escape out the front gate she is off in a flash.

With her great charm and ability to manipulate people she is never short of human companions, so can happily accept a new owner if circumstances decree.

The Gemini canine needs a lot of rest, but is unlikely to be able to sleep when she needs it most, as her twin likes to keep her on the move. Unfortunately she is inclined to suffer from mental exhaustion, usually brought about by an overflow of nervous energy, and this in turn can create a host of problems associated with stress. She is susceptible to accidents and infections, and during her lifetime will probably have numerous visits to the vet for one complaint or another. A lot of Geminis will also develop a tendency to bite, and if you have small children ready to torment your pet when she is trying to relax, it should come as no surprise to see the darker side of her nature emerge. Unable to tolerate unfairness, she is likely to react swiftly and without thought for any consequent punishment.

The Gemini dog enjoys chasing the postman, considering this to be a satisfactory way of relieving built-up tension.

Her quick intelligence helps her solve all sorts of problems, and because she also possesses a native cunning and slyness of manner she is often underhand in her actions. It is not against her principles to visit the local school to steal the children's lunches. Paradoxically, she can also be honest to a

enjoys chasing the postman

21

fault and may express her guilt in a most charming manner, especially if there is displeasure all around.

Like any creature with the air as her element, this animal's feet are rarely on the ground and she never really finds her heart's desire, though she seeks it constantly.

A Gemini's emotions do not run too deeply, as her inner self, her other ego, is her closest companion, and she tends to hide her true motives from others.

Even though she has an ability to make friends easily, the Gemini forgets these same friends just as quickly if parted from them for any length of time. However, she is rarely jealous of those who get more attention than she, and has little inclination to be possessive toward her owner or property. Her very airiness, fickleness and unpredictability do not make her the perfect watchdog or loyal companion, as she will never give all of herself to anyone.

Gemini dogs usually live well into old age. They are inclined, however, to have trouble with the digestive organs, bronchial tubes and upper part of the lungs. This can make them subject to pneumonia and the canine born under the sign of Gemini is better protected from illnesses if she has somewhere quiet to eat her dinner and is kept warm at night.

Your pet enjoys the sensation of speed and can be a nuisance in the car, as she tends to jump about. This is most disconcerting for the driver as the dog remains in a perpetual state of excitement when travelling.

She readily accepts a puppy as a companion, though it is advisable to pair her with one born under a compatible sign.

Like the Piscean, the Gemini dog can behave in a way exactly the opposite to that which you have been led to expect, and goes from one extreme to the other. Sometimes an outing on the beach will cause her to bound into the water and show great exuberance of spirit, whereas on other occasions she refuses to acknowledge the very existence of the elements that gave her so much pleasure previously. Her unpredictability can cause havoc in the home, and if boredom cannot be relieved, treasured items may be vandalised. Whether it be chewed items of clothing or scratched furniture, remember it is your Gemini dog showing displeasure with a life that has become too routine.

By the same token, this pet can usually escape your wrath by putting on a convincing performance of one wrongly accused in the hope of gaining immediate forgiveness. It also gives her the opportunity to show off her acting ability, and thus avoid severe punishment.

The Gemini dog looks best wearing a collar that is either silver or glistening white.

Your canine will find the most lasting friendships either with others born during this period, or with those whose signs are Libra, Aquarius or Sagittarius.

Paltry Pilaf

No matter what you serve your Gemini dog at mealtimes, it is unlikely that she will readily show her appreciation of your culinary skills, for food is not always a priority with this animal. Therefore I have chosen Paltry Pilaf in the hope that it might become a favourite dish, and one that can be served regularly. The pasta provides the necessary bulk to refuel your pet's energy levels, and the cooked chicken pieces, embraced by the oil and breadcrumbs, will be easy to digest. Because canines born under the sign of Gemini are prone to digestive disorders, the old adage, 'forewarned is forearmed' holds true when dealing with a Gemini. To understand her personality is to understand her digestive system, and sensible eating in a quiet environment can bring many a renegade to heel.

cooked chicken pieces   *½ cup breadcrumbs*
pasta (any variety will do)   *polyunsaturated oil*

Boil the pasta until it is *al dente*, firm rather than soft. Drain, and whilst it is cooling strip the meat from the chicken bones. These must be discarded, lest they splinter and then cause damage to the intestinal tract. Toss the chicken pieces into the pasta, add the oil and prepared breadcrumbs. The breadcrumbs help elevate this recipe above the realm of the ordinary.

CANCER

The zodiacal sign of Cancer commences on 21 June, but does not come into full power until on or about 28 June. The sign of Cancer, or the Crab, was so called by early man because the sun at this time of the year appears to advance and retreat in the sky, recalling the movements of a crab.

The Cancerian dog's passing moods are often in rhythm with the phases of the moon, so the caring owner must realise that this pet's personality will be governed by fluctuating highs and lows, just as the moon waxes and wanes in the heavens above. Shall I suggest that the Cancerian animal is consistent in his inconsistency? An understanding person probably will have no trouble recognising these phases, and one hopes will not be troubled by changing moods and emotions.

He is a great home-lover, this dog of yours, therefore usually can be found lying by the hearth, or on the most comfortable sofa. On the other hand, he can be compelled by an unexplainable restlessness, and a desire to search the inner depths of his soul for something he can never reach. Do not be too surprised if the pet born under this sign tends to roam at random, unless confined to his territory. During these periods of soul-searching, distant fields are always greener than the grass at home. The Cancerian dog can develop strong territorial instincts, and woe betide anyone or anything that sets foot inside his gate without being invited. Your pet adapts very well to a sudden change

25

of environment; this may appear contradictory, as the love of one's home is the strongest trait of those born during the sign of the Crab.

The Cancer dog has a loving and affectionate disposition, but does not like being chastised, or dictated to, for he possesses a very sensitive nature. He becomes easily depressed, and needs to be given encouragement and praise for his efforts as much as possible. He is seldom demonstrative, preferring his owner to make the first overtures of affection. One is sometimes inclined to pass him off as being cold and unemotional, but nothing is further from the truth. Secretly the Cancer canine really enjoys attention, preferring to bask in occasional adulation without seeking the centre of the stage.

When this pet becomes depressed his mood can enfold you, and as he has so many intense moods, he is unable to feel completely secure within himself; consequently some Cancer dogs wear pessimistic expressions on their faces for most of their lives.

If the dog's security is threatened, the ensuing depression can often make him quite sick. His vulnerable areas are the chest, kidneys, bladder and skin; a lot of his time can be spent scratching if he is unfortunate enough to be plagued by eczema. The owner will find that when the pet is gloomy it does no good making a fuss of him; the animal might court sympathy, but at the same time does not want anyone to feel sorry for him. Like the Crab, he tends to retreat into his shell until it is safe to come out. The Cancerian dog's nature contains areas of fragility and vulnerability; unable to shake off criticism, he finds his only defence is to withdraw into his own world and deny access to others.

He is capable of bearing a grudge for a considerable period, and tends to remember the bad times more than the good. Like the crab, he occasionally resorts to being snappy and irritable with those he loves, preferring to regret his actions at leisure, for this can sometimes be used as an excuse to enjoy a period of sulkiness.

The Cancerian canine never forgets any lessons he has learned. You might notice he possesses amazing recall of events that would appear to be well and truly forgotten. He can be very secretive, and guards his true inner feelings from those around him.

This pet likes to have time to reflect and analyse, rather than commit himself to an immediate decision that he might be expected to act upon without thought for the outcome.

The dog born under this sign can be very tenacious, and because of his constant feelings of insecurity is likely to be a hoarder. He buries his bones, rather than chewing on them when they are presented to him, just in case he is at some later stage left without food.

As the crab can walk backwards, forwards and sideways with great agility, so does your pet, so much so that he never goes directly after what he wants. By observing him, you will see that he can play a waiting game, and his tenacity will eventually prove itself in this manner. The Cancer canine is not always very brave; he would rather see others take the initiative in decision-making unless his territory is threatened. Then he becomes braver in his actions, so one cannot accuse him of cowardice on these occasions.

A Cancerian pet loves water, and does not have to be encouraged to swim or wade to his heart's content; regardless of the weather he is always ready to immerse himself completely. Another contradiction appears here, as the dog born during the sign of Cancer is not necessarily a good swimmer, and can sometimes literally get into deep water. He is unlikely to panic, even if on the verge of drowning, because he feels he belongs to the element completely.

A Cancer dog usually excels at obedience training, owing to a willingness to learn, helped also by being gifted with a

27

A Cancerian pet loves water . . . he feels he belongs to the element completely

splendid memory. This can make it a most enjoyable and rewarding experience for both the pet and the owner. Because of his tendency to react unfavourably to criticism, training must be given carefully, with praise heaped upon him, or again the pet will withdraw into his shell, sometimes undermining the good foundations already laid.

There is a touch of moon madness in all Cancerian dogs; your pet might start barking at night for no apparent reason, or whine and whimper at the door when he has just asked to be put outside. The canine born during this sign gets a certain pleasure from howling at the full moon, but is genuinely frightened by electrical storms and fireworks. Consequently, the dog is not very relaxing to live with, and you could spend a lot of time catering to his every whim.

As he has the capacity to absorb everything he wants to know about you, he is naturally able to take advantage of any personal weaknesses, thus enjoying a very pampered life.

The most lasting friendships are found with other dogs born under this sign, or with Scorpio, Capricorn and Pisces dogs.

A Cancerian dog is most suited to green, cream and white, as background colours that will enhance his personality.

Bluey's Broth

The following recipe should really suit a Cancerian dog if he is prone to eczema, or has bladder problems. The power of barley as a palliative is well recorded, and throughout history it has been used to treat a variety of complaints. The ancient Egyptians grew it, as did the Greeks, Romans and Chinese.

For working dogs especially, this dish is hard to beat — not only does the dog benefit from the contents of the broth, but the shank bones can be regarded as an added bonus. Around campfires across Australia you will find many a sheep dog anxiously waiting for his share of the broth to cool, and those who have camped along the trail will probably recognise this dish as authentic Aussie fare — definitely a dish that lends itself well to a cold winter's night.

2 lamb shanks	*1 chopped onion (optional)*
1 cup barley	*1 cup chopped cabbage*
1 grated potato	*1 cup freshly shelled peas*
2 beef cubes	*½ cup grated pumpkin*

Cover shanks with water, bring to the boil, pour off water and start again. This process removes grit and any other impurities from the meat. Add barley and simmer for 20 minutes before stirring in the vegetables and cooking for a further 20 minutes. Remove shanks, strip meat and add to soup.

Your dog will no doubt enjoy this when it is cool, but if you have any reservations I would suggest some is poured over his dried food. Most working dogs relish this broth and my blue heeler, though an unemployed canine, is no exception.

THE LION

LEO

The zodiacal sign of Leo commences on 21 July, but does not come into its full power until on or about 28 July.

The Leo dog is a warm and generous creature, possessing a somewhat naive arrogance that cannot be ignored. She is a canine who walks proudly, displaying an almost feline grace that lends dignity to her purposeful stride.

At home the Leo pet likes to take advantage of all the comforts available, so can usually be found reclining on the leather sofa, or stretched out on an imported rug. If your house caters to more humble tastes, and has a nicely lived-in feel about it, never mind, as Leo with her regal demeanour will manage to bring a touch of elegance to any room.

Occasionally the Leo dog develops an insufferable ego, probably because it is easy to spoil her without really being aware of doing so — few could resist a pet with such a lovable nature, and the capacity to forgive in a matter of minutes. If she is the type of dog who has become selfish or dictatorial, through getting her own way too often, or if she seems inclined to challenge your authority, exceptionally firm control must be exercised, with rewards meted out only when earned. It is important that she is taught to respect others.

Do not overlook the importance attached to offering praise to the dog when it is deserved, as her heart will be won forever, nothing soothes Leo more effectively than flattery. It acts as

with her regal demeanour will bring a touch of elegance to any room

a balm to her soul, and a stimulant to her senses. Outgoing as she appears, this canine is very vulnerable, with a desperate need to be loved and a terrible fear of rejection. When expected praise is not forthcoming, moody, sulky behaviour might result, followed by a downward slide into deep melancholia. Usually such periods of depression are brief — Leo can bounce back quickly, having the capacity to take the good times with the bad. Rarely introverted, your pet shows her feelings for all to see.

It is rare for this canine to lose her sense of dignity, and she is always aware of her position in life. She is most astute, and has the intelligence to predict her position in the household with great accuracy. If the odds are not in Leo's favour, she is always very prompt in trying to amend the situation. Your dog has a considerable amount of wisdom, but her vanity can override many other attributes. Providing she maintains a balanced judgement and keeps her ego in check, a better companion could not be found.

The Leo dog is of course lion-hearted, and can be relied upon to protect the home with tenacity and loyalty. She is also utterly fearless, patrolling her territory with the air of a monarch despatching favours to chosen subjects. It is advisable for visitors not to argue with a Leo pet.

Among her peers she stands out as a natural leader. This even applies to smaller Leo dogs — rarely are they challenged on the basis of size alone. If she is forced to fight, aggression lends added strength to the confidence this animal has in tackling a rival. Because the Leo pet knows no fear, she refuses to acknowledge defeat unless all her resources are depleted. With such a fiery disposition, the dog is inclined to act impetuously at times, especially if the proper respect is not forthcoming.

The canine born during the sign of Leo prefers fresh, raw meat to anything else, and is likely to turn away from tainted food. As she is basically very fixed in nature, it can be difficult sometimes to tempt her with new foods, or to hide any medication in her meat, as she unerringly knows when something is different.

A playful dog, Leo takes time to mature, so puppy habits are retained well into middle years. Her energy can be boundless, but she refuses to waste time on unimportant matters. When visitors are introduced to your pet they are often overwhelmed by the greeting, so the larger Leo animal is better left in the back garden when guests are expected.

This canine is at her best during the day, even though a large portion of her waking hours are spent in idleness. With fire as her element, the Leo animal craves the sunshine; she is rarely adversely affected by the heat, but on a warm day when the wind is blowing strongly the animal prefers to remain indoors. Normally she is content to find a spot in the garden unaffected by shade, thus giving her the full benefit of the sun's rays.

Once night has fallen the pet born during the sign of Leo does not waste time baying at the moon. She considers herself to be superior to other canines, and would like to win praise for her prowess as a leader and ability to look after the pack.

The Leo dog rarely gets flustered, nor is she prone to panic if left alone to protect the property, so can cope with most situations. She has the power to inspire and instil confidence in all she meets, but is attracted most to those possessing the same strength of character. Lasting friendships are formed with other Leos, and with Aries, Capricorn and Sagittarian dogs.

Leo is inclined to strain on the lead when out walking, so one must be fairly fit to keep up with this animal. Always an attention-seeker, your pet will cause heads to turn in her direction if wearing a jewelled collar, as befitting a canine born during the sign of Leo. All shades of yellow, orange, pale green and white complement this regal pet's appearance.

Even though you may occasionally be embarrassed by Leo's exuberance and desire to be noticed, she is rarely depressing company, but a worthy pet prepared to do her utmost to make your day brighter.

Mongrel Meat Medley

Because the Leo dog is not always prepared to try anything new, wait until she is really hungry before you experiment with different foods. I am sure this recipe, with its distinctive meaty aroma, would be most acceptable to her. She should relish the nutty taste of the barley as it slides down her throat, and look upon the bones as a bonus. If she appears hesitant the first time you offer her Mongrel Meat Medley, add a little chopped meat to it. Appealing to her vanity works wonders, and praise is the ultimate reward when looking to succeed with the Leo pet.

The origins of this recipe are shrouded in mystery, but as far as I can ascertain it was at the height of its popularity during the Middle Ages. Eventually it fell from favour amongst the aristocracy and became confined to the lower classes. As it is both an economical and sustaining dish for your dog, I feel it warrants a mention here.

2 lamb flaps/neck of lamb	*1 ox heart*
¾ cup barley	*a pinch of herbs*

Put all ingredients in a saucepan and barely cover with water. Make sure the lid is on the saucepan to suppress the odour given off whilst cooking, then simmer gently for 30 minutes. When cool, remove the ox heart and chop into bite-size pieces. Return to the saucepan with the other ingredients and before serving to your dog, place two slices of brown bread in her dish to absorb juices. If the liquid has not sufficiently reduced during cooking I would suggest you drain some off.

VIRGO

The zodiacal sign of Virgo commences on 21 August, but does not come into its full power until or about 28 August.

If your dog was born during this period it does not automatically mean that you have a pure and chaste pet. Unfortunately, Virgos are more capable of going to extremes in good and evil than any other type, and they can develop a cunning and crafty side to their nature. Nevertheless, even if this happens the animal manages to wear a mantle of purity and innocence most convincingly, allowing only a chosen few to gain a glimpse of his true self.

The Virgo canine is inclined to be undemonstrative, preferring to give love quietly and faithfully, without being unduly lavish in his affections. Remember, he does not want to feel obligated in any way, even to his owner, and because of a very practical nature, dislikes people who are gushy, noisy and insincere. As he tends to exude a quiet charm, and unconsciously wears a serene expression on his face, your pet sometimes unwittingly encourages friendships when he does not wish to.

Underneath a seemingly calm exterior lies a nervous intensity of manner, consequently the Virgo dog is unable to relax as much as he should; excessive mental stimulation can debilitate him rapidly, so that he will refuse to participate in normal activities if stressed. Virgo produces a far greater percentage of hypochondriacs than any other sign, these animals are great

36

a far greater percentage of hypochondriacs than any other sign

worriers, often falling prey to all sorts of ills, either real or imagined. Unnecessary worry might cause stomach and liver disorders, there is also a tendency towards arthritis in later years, but generally those born during this sign enjoy excellent health, managing to retain a youthful appearance throughout life.

The Virgo dog is inclined to be over-fastidious in regards to personal hygiene, indeed it is not uncommon for him to develop a fetish about cleanliness, he may well constantly lick his paws until raw patches develop. Other parts of the body could also suffer the same fate if the pet is a chronic nibbler.

Your canine is sometimes a selective eater, so one must pander to his occasional whims, because he will prefer to go hungry rather than dine on food which is distasteful to him. His delicate exterior belies an inner toughness and strength, but because of such an obsession with health, it is unlikely the animal will neglect his body to any extent.

The Virgo pet is a true child of nature; if a city dog, he needs plenty of fresh air and sunlight, and has a preference for regular outings in the country. When feeling out of sorts, the canine becomes nervous, cranky and short-tempered, sometimes it is advisable to give him time to recharge his physical and mental batteries by banishing him to a quiet corner. Make sure this is done in a most tactful manner, so as not to create feelings of rejection and exclusion from the family circle.

As we have seen, the hyperactive part of the Virgo dog's nature creates tension within, so an uncluttered, peaceful environment is of great benefit to your pet. Because he is such a creature of habit, most upsets occur if the routine of life is suddenly altered, even in the slightest way. Harmony in the home is essential, any shouting or fighting amongst the children causes the animal to move well away from the source of the trouble. His digestion is easily upset by changes within the home, therefore moving the furniture or allocating another area for him to sleep in might cause worry and distress.

The Virgo canine possesses an excellent memory, coupled with an inbuilt sense of punctuality. He likes his meal at the exact same time each day, knowing almost to the minute when it is due. He is capable of meeting the school bus, and escorting the children home, so it seems nothing is impossible for this animal to learn. His eyes are usually soft and gentle and full of intelligence. To teach him, though, requires patience and understanding, as he cannot fully cope with criticism, no matter how constructive it might be.

Because your dog's ego needs regular bolstering to maintain

self-esteem, constant references to his cleverness produces marvellous results. To be reprimanded hurts his pride, though he can be very stubborn when asked to perform a task unpleasant to him, this is when a little bribery might go a long way in achieving better results.

A pet born during the sign of Virgo is inclined to be a loner among his own kind, but he is very considerate of smaller and weaker animals. With a strong desire to uphold law and order he can instinctively restore peace to an unruly pack. He respects leadership qualities in other dogs, but does not crave this position for himself, being happy to mediate when necessary.

Female Virgos make good mothers, passing on many basic skills to their young with exceptional efficiency. Once the pups are self-sufficient the Virgo bitch might quickly abandon them; as she herself craves independence, so she values it in others.

I would like to touch lightly on the darker side of the Virgo nature, which as I mentioned earlier, can go to extremes in good and evil. Occasionally one encounters such a pet, possibly it might so happen that the puppy which wreaks havoc in the home and remains undisciplined grows to be cunning and crafty at the expense of others. As an adult, this dog manages to cover up his lapses exceedingly well, so is rarely banished from the family circle. His charm, dazzling in its intensity, usually wins over even the most outspoken critics.

To complement his personality, the Virgo dog needs to be surrounded by soft, cool colours and is more inclined to gravitate towards the ferns than the flower beds.

Virgo pets appear to form lasting friendships with those born under their own sign, but a compatibility exists also with Taurus, Aries, Capricorn and Pisces dogs.

Royal Rump

Even the most fastidious Virgo dog will not refuse to eat this dish, unless he is ill. It was very popular during the reign of King Charles II and fed regularly to the royal spaniels. If you cannot afford to buy rump steak on a regular basis, I would suggest a cheaper cut of meat as an alternative. Though exceptionally fussy, the Virgo canine is sure to accept a substitution for rump if the meal is nicely presented. With Virgo, one must focus on the stomach and liver, as the digestive system is inclined to be delicate. Therefore, bland food is preferable to spicy, and too high a fat content in the diet might create unwanted problems. The addition of carrot and parsley not only provides your pet with extra vitamins and roughage, but visual interest as well — the importance of eye appeal cannot be overlooked.

1 lean piece rump steak   *2 rashers bacon (cooked)*
½ grated carrot   *chopped parsley*

Cut steak into bite-size pieces, then sprinkle with the grated carrot, crumbled bacon and chopped parsley. Arrange neatly on your best china plate, as presentation is most important in order to maintain the high standard associated with this recipe.

LIBRA

The zodiacal sign of Libra commences on 21 September, but does not come into full power until on or about 28 September.

The sign of Libra is symbolised by the golden scales of Justice, so that the dog born during this period is likely to be well balanced. An air of serenity hangs about her and a feeling of sweetness and light is there on her face for all to see. Consequently this pet endears herself to many, certainly it would be hard to find a better companion. Probably her most sought-after and talked about quality is trustworthiness. Rarely do you hear of a Libran canine that bites the children or chases the cat; even when angry she somehow manages to retain a pleasant expression on her face.

Your dog avoids trouble as much as she possibly can, and usually has a favourite place of retreat if the younger members of the family become too boisterous in their play, or the cat decides to torment her. The Libran pet has a great love of people, but a fear of crowds; though she might crave human company, it is impossible for her to retain a balanced state of mind when hemmed in by others.

Because Libra hates to be rude, the canine born under this sign spends a lot of time trying to please everyone by behaving in a good-natured manner. Observe her overall appearance and you might notice curves rather than angles are responsible for the softness of expression found upon her features and the contours of her limbs.

41

curves rather than angles are responsible for the softness of her features and the contours of her limbs

The Libran dog excels at keeping peace and harmony alive within her group of canine acquaintances. You no doubt will become conversant with her ability to defend territory without actually engaging in a fight, as those born during this period hate bloodshed, and try to avoid it at all costs. Again the tendency is there to weigh and analyse, and this, coupled with a gentle disposition, makes the pet a mediator rather than a combatant.

I would like to touch on the subject of the Libran's psychic abilities, even though a lot of readers will be inclined to dismiss this as nonsense. The animal is certainly capable of anticipating events within the household before they occur, and if anyone is feeling ill, she is the first to offer loyalty and companionship to the patient. She also has an uncanny knack of being at the front door to greet visitors before they have even set foot inside the front gate.

Harmony in all aspects of life is most sought after by this canine, active spells must be alternated with periods of complete rest. The dog is normally capable of maintaining a delicate balance between her physical and mental needs but periods of depression occasionally do occur, making the pet morose and stubborn, even to the point where she will refuse to obey an order. These moods affect her health, consequently the skin can become itchy and the feet sore, though this is more noticeable in older Libran dogs.

The survival instinct is very strong with Libra, therefore the animal works harder than most at keeping herself youthful and mentally alert. 'Lazy Libra' is a term often applicable to this sign, lethargy sits well upon the Libran pet until she feels a spurt of energy which activates her once more into living life at a steady, even pace.

Libra is not a dual sign, though you could be forgiven for thinking so if your dog is one whose scales are tipped and impossible to balance for the time being. She will never have the resources available to completely change character, as with the Gemini, but swings strongly from one emotion to the other. Therefore, it is possible for the canine to be quarrelsome, stubborn, restless and confused during these particular periods.

Because the Libra dog moves within the changing element of air, she picks up the vibrations that flow all around her, although her strong need for logic can negate this power.

If members of her household tend to act rashly or impulsively too often, the ensuing vibrations are picked up by the Libran pet, causing her to be nervous and indecisive. I have shown you how important balance is to this dog, so it is rare to see erratic behaviour lasting for any length of time. Providing she can adjust her scales accordingly, the animal returns to being her normal, easy self, though an unexpected outburst of anger from a member of the family, whether directed at her or not, can once more rock the delicate mechanism of Libra.

As she is usually extremely intelligent, the Libran dog can concentrate exceedingly well when taken to obedience classes, but must be allowed to take some time to absorb knowledge, needing to weigh all the pros and cons. Having done this she retains the information so accurately that the lesson does not have to be constantly repeated, as with some pupils.

Music can help create a harmonious mood within the Libran pet's home, the sounds borne upon the air are a balm to her soul and poetry to her ears. No dog sniffs the breeze more keenly, or acts upon the direction of a certain scent more positively, than Libra; remember this is her element, sure to satisfy her senses and form lasting impressions in her mind.

The desire to be loved beats strongly within your canine's breast, though she is not an animal to approach all and sundry for a pat or a kind word. She welcomes the assurance that she is held in high regard by members of the household, rather than the public. Because her manners are so impeccable, she is not likely to be found fawning or grovelling at anyone's feet as a means of gaining attention. The Libran dog prefers to let her owner make the first overtures of affection, but again, any overly generous displays of love can cause the pet embarrassment. Libra craves peace and happiness, so needs to be shown as often as possible, without fuss, that her position in the home is just as important as anyone else's.

A change of address is sometimes a major upheaval for your dog; those born during the sign of Libra seem unable to cope with drastic changes within their environment, and a long time can be taken in adapting to a new home.

The Libran pet, with her sweet expression, looks particularly good wearing a blue collar; any shade of this colour is suitable, but do not overlook violet, purple or mauve as colours complementary to her appearance.

Friendships are best formed with those born during the same sign, or Aquarius, Gemini and Aries dogs.

Liver is Wurst

The name given to this dish is a misnomer, for most cooks are aware that liver, when well presented, is a culinary delight. Its apparent unpopularity could be due to the fact that few restaurants bother about it at all, and modern cook books rely on glossy coloured photos of exotic food to titillate their reader's taste buds. After an upsetting experience with liver in a local cafe, one wit has presented me with the title 'Liver is Wurst'. He was forced to bring home the remains of his meal in a doggy bag, but to his amazement, the family's bull mastiff wolfed it down in seconds.

The Libran dog should avoid over-eating, for obesity will create problems with the feet and skin as the animal ages. An occasional meal of liver adds balance to the existing diet, and being virtually fat free, is easy to digest if well cooked. Baking it in the oven minimises unpleasant odours and the addition of crushed garlic puts it in a class of its own.

1 calf liver   *chopped parsley*
polyunsaturated oil

Smear oil generously over liver, then place on a baking tray. Bake in a moderate oven for approximately 30 minutes, but if still pink, return for a little longer — all offal should be well cooked, and liver is no exception. Chop the liver into bite-size pieces and neatly arrange on the dog's dish. Garnish with parsley and serve.

This makes for a satisfying and nutritious meal. If you have a large dog to feed, I would suggest the addition of dried food. In combination with the liver, an interesting texture results.

THE SCORPION

SCORPIO

The zodiacal sign of Scorpio commences on 21 October, but does not come into its full power until on or about 28 October.

The dog born during this sign is often contradictory in nature, thus making it difficult for you to find the true essence of Scorpio. Some pets are extremely pure-minded in thought, therefore, a sweetness of spirit is reflected in their eyes, endearing them to all. Others have the tendency to be extremely selfish, expecting favours from all quarters, and are usually vengeful in outlook if wronged.

Scorpio is represented by two symbols, namely the Scorpion and the Eagle, so your pet can follow either, or lie somewhere in between. If he chooses to imitate the eagle he will soar to great heights, overcoming obstacles in his path fearlessly, but always on the lookout for easy prey. The Scorpio dog may be unpredictable and difficult to fathom at times, but it would be a mistake to compare him too closely with the symbol his sign represents. It was originally thought that the scorpion would sting itself to death if encircled by fire, and interestingly enough some pets born during this sign certainly regard fire with superstition and awe. Most prefer to relax in a quiet corner, rather than seek the warmth of the heater or the intimacy of an open hearth in winter.

Scorpio dogs are quiet animals, but possess an inner turbulence which is so well contained that it rarely surfaces. Your canine probably manages to conceal his emotions admirably, only allowing you an occasional glimpse of his true inner self. There is no disguising the vitality which animates the Scorpio pet, however, or his intense interest in life; often these factors compel him to seek adventure far from home.

You may be at a loss sometimes to ascertain his needs, for he can fix you with a hypnotic stare, probing your soul in a most disconcerting way, without a change of expression. When least expected, this animal permits a trace of a smile to flit across his features, otherwise little indication is given of any true feelings. The pet's ego is inviolate, as there is no need to prove himself to others. He has supreme confidence in his own ability to withstand the rigours of his existence.

The Scorpio dog enjoys receiving affection from those he loves, his loyalty is without question, and he shows unfailing courage if forced to protect the household from danger. Sometimes one is deceived by his outwardly gentle manner, for deep inside this canine lurks a toughness and determination that cannot be undermined. Scorpio is possessive to a fault, an irritating habit at times, especially if he chooses to be jealous of those you converse with.

The pet born under this sign is an exceptional watchdog, but has a tendency to be sneaky in his approach. Consequently strangers are often taken by surprise, for the animal hides his true motives. The average Scorpio is content to retain a low profile, away from the limelight, therefore he is unlikely to pose a threat to accepted friends.

One of Scorpio's worst faults is his inclination to be influenced strongly by those he comes into contact with — he sometimes adapts too easily to unsuitable companions. If he is in the company of his owner for most of the day, a blending of personalities may occur, so that both parties are able to live in complete harmony, rarely disagreeing. Though Scorpio tries to control his emotions as much as possible, praise is appreciated and gratefully acknowledged, often with an unexpected wag of the tail or some other gesture of affection. Reprimands are treated with a certain amount of contempt, and if chastised too severely this dog does not readily forgive. Exposing any faults your pet might harbour can present difficulties, for he believes so truly in himself that he does not like to be shown personal shortcomings, and is liable to take offence.

In a crisis the Scorpio dog can usually be relied upon to remain calm, somehow he draws on hidden reserves to cope with the problems of others. He is not the type of animal to be daunted by an electrical storm, so is useful when the children are frightened by thunder. Intense emotion and cool logic jockey for control of the Scorpio psyche, but more often than not they remain compatible bedfellows, depending on the need of the moment.

With a propensity to be extremely brave, the dog born during this sign dislikes fighting unless provoked, but once aroused is impervious to pain. He either makes friends or enemies instantly, is single-minded in his determination to eliminate a foe, and tracks an enemy relentlessly, never content to let the argument rest.

For some Scorpios, the sweet taste of victory is overshadowed by the desire for further revenge. This causes a regression of spirit within the dog, unless he is able to rise above his fixation, to soar skywards with the eagle.

If you have the misfortune to be sick or upset, it is the Scorpio canine who offers his condolences more readily than any other, being prepared to sacrifice his time to lie quietly near you. Again, one must never question his loyalty, as he is prepared to give what he has of himself to those he loves.

This dog has an affinity with the sea, so if you have access to the water he will relish every moment spent on the beach, regardless of the weather. Observe how he chases the wheeling, teasing gulls until ready to drop at your feet in a state of joyous exhaustion. Your pet welcomes the changes each season brings, and has an exceptional awareness of the cycles of life.

an exceptional watchdog but has a tendency to be sneaky in his approach . . . has an affinity with the sea

Good health is usually experienced by Scorpio, without him having to worry about obesity in later life. Areas prone to disease are the reproductive organs and kidneys. The heart may weaken if overtaxed by excessive exercise, so watch those outings on the beach. Problems do sometimes occur in the region of the back, causing weakness to the legs.

As friendships are treasured, it is important this dog retains certain companions to spend time with; constant isolation tends to bring out the worst in him.

Your pet touches others with his quiet vitality, friends respect him but are wary of overstepping too many boundaries when in his company. Most favoured friendships are to be found with other Scorpios, and with Cancer, Pisces and Taurus dogs.

Colours best suited to the dog born under this sign are all shades of crimson and blue.

Terrier's Tripe & Shepherd's Sauce

As a child I can clearly remember the local rat-catcher and his team of fox terriers; these wiry and tenacious little animals were adept at flushing out and then killing their quarry. The rat-catcher often joked about the food he prepared for his dogs, and asserted that if he ate it himself it was good enough for his workers. The mincemeat belongs to the original recipe, and acts as a stimulant to the taste buds. It also adds colour to a seemingly bland dish. The Scorpio pet is intelligent enough to recognise the effort you have made in managing to prepare and cook the tripe without incident. The task can be a formidable one, as most people abhor handling tripe, but others also object to the odours that arise from the pot when it is simmering on the stove. I think the end result is worthwhile, for the Scorpio dog never forgets, and will forever show his appreciation in countless subtle ways.

tripe according to appetite   *½ grated carrot*
small quantity beef mince   *1 egg*
1 tablespoon fat

Simmer tripe for 20 minutes in water; retain one cupful of the resulting liquid and drain off the excess. Chop the tripe into bite-size pieces and place in a dish to cool. To make the sauce, lightly brown the meat in the fat. Remove the mixture from the stove, and add the grated carrot and lightly beaten egg to the meat before finally stirring in the cupful of liquid. Pour the sauce over the tripe and serve to an appreciative pet.

THE ARCHER

SAGITTARIUS

The zodiacal sign of Sagittarius commences on 21 November, but does nto come into its full power until on or about 28 November.

The Sagittarian dog is a lovable, though tactless, canine who delights in drawing attention to herself at the most inopportune moments. She sometimes achieves this through lavish displays of affection, but an unconcealed eagerness to please can be badly timed, as the directness of her approach does not take into account the moods and feelings of others.

Your pet often decides to be boisterous when least expected, and if allowed the freedom of the house is capable of acting in such an exuberant manner that one has no choice but to put her outside. Though unaware of the effect her presence has on visitors in particular, if chastised for any misdemeanours she is able to accept the punishment with quiet resignation, which belies a reckless attitude to life.

This canine normally has a happy disposition, and appears to harbour no malice in her soul toward others. The Sagittarian never anticipates trouble, expecting to remain friends with everyone, but the bluntness of her approach often causes rebuffs when introductions are made. As there is nothing hesitant about your dog, discretion is usually lacking when it is needed most. Because of her lack of caution, her penchant for dangerous situations, newly formed friendships are often pushed to the limit.

Because your pet channels most of her energies towards whatever she is doing at a particular moment, it is difficult to gain her attention once she has found something of interest. She is apt to be single-minded in the pursuit of new scents, and such investigations tend to find her wandering a long way from home.

Most Sagittarians are regarded as reliable custodians of children, because dishonest or deceitful behaviour is rarely associated with those born under this sign. An aura of trust-worthiness speaks for itself, and tactless though she may be, your canine is basically sincere.

To recognise a healthy Sagittarian dog, find one whose eyes shine brightly, expressing the humour and intelligence within. She is ordinarily a playful pet with a mischievous streak that asserts itself as often as possible. It would be difficult to remain annoyed with the animal for any length of time, as she literally bounces with enthusiasm and well-being. Expressive body language conveys to others the understanding of the spoken word; many facets of a conversation if directed toward a Sagittarian, are correctly interpreted and acted upon. Her personality is sometimes overpowering — her vitality sweeps others along in its path.

The dog's awkwardness and lack of grace are accentuated by her desire to hurry from one project to the next, in the hope that by the end of the day all areas of interest will have been thoroughly examined. You may find this canine's restlessness occasionally disrupts the pattern of the household, as consider-able time could be spent helping her decide whether to stay indoors or venture outside to enjoy the serenity of the garden.

Because she is such a friendly, sociable creature, the animal sometimes regards her own environment as a prison, if others are not there to share it. Often by gaining another pet you can solve the problem, but at first you will have to curb her enthusiasm for the newcomer. Eventually the sincerity of your dog's welcome will overcome prior apprehensions. The protective nature of Sagittarius is all-enveloping, and though she is over-possessive at times, there is never any feeling of insecurity while she is around, for her loyalty towards loved ones is constant.

Nearly always an extrovert, the canine born during this sign is sometimes capable of outrageous behaviour, especially when in a capricious mood. As I mentioned earlier, she delights in monopolising your company and can expertly manipulate a situation to procure a titbit or have her stomach scratched.

inclined to be accident-prone

The Sagittarian dog is inclined to be accident-prone, but has a reluctance to seek sympathy for minor injuries, knowing that if she were more careful mishaps might be avoided. Luckily this pet is blessed with reasonable traffic sense, so the majority of accidents are likely to be of a lesser nature and are usually associated with cuts to the feet. Sagittarius is drawn into dangerous situations like a moth to a flame; the element of risk prompts the flow of adrenalin, lessening her chances of reacting to pain or discomfort of any kind, so she is often unaware of hazards underfoot as she races off in pursuit of her quarry. A lot of energy is dispersed by the animal during the course of a day. Because she looks forward to tomorrow with enthusiasm, it is unlikely you will find her giving in to sickness, unless it is of a serious nature. Trouble spots are the lungs, liver, intestines, feet and legs, but as your dog treats pain with stoicism, it can be difficult to gauge the seriousness of a complaint. Moody spells are short-lived, for the optimism of the Sagittarian dog guarantees that periods of depression are rare, and quickly dispelled.

Because your pet has a remarkably good memory, her awareness of life is all the more acute, as lessons are not easily forgotten. She prefers to take life as it comes, and fortified by this attitude rarely becomes senile, retaining an enviable youthfulness.

If for any reason your Sagittarian canine has to be left in the care of others, she can be relied upon to adjust quickly to a strange household, providing she is met with kindness. Confidence and adaptability are important factors to be considered if one leads a nomadic lifestyle and seeks a pet that will fit into this way of life. The spirit of Sagittarius is free, burning brightly to show she is answerable to no one.

The dog looks fetching against a backdrop of all shades of mauve and violet, highlighting her healthy appearance.

Most lasting friendships are formed with others born under the same sign, or under Aries, Leo and Gemini.

RECIPE

Early Settlers' Stew

The Sagittarian dog accepts most food put in front of her, and with a propensity for good health, should live out her allotted life span if sensibly fed. Because this animal is constantly on the move, she has to eat a lot to sustain her energy. The ingredients in the stew are guaranteed to retain the gloss on her coat and the bounce in her step. Some dogs born during this period have more grace and style than others, but most hurry through each day as if their lives depended on it. Consequently, food tends to be eaten too quickly. The following recipe is chosen with Sagittarius in mind, as it is hoped the vegetables will heighten her curiosity and slow her down a little. Finally, I would suggest serving Early Settlers' Stew in a deep bowl so as to capture the full essence of the dish, and ensure that none of the juices are lost. Most dogs enjoy it, though some will reject the pumpkin.

6 chump chops	*stick of celery*
2 potatoes	*4 pieces pumpkin*
1 carrot	*1 onion*
a little flour	*1 cup water*

Coat chops with flour and brown in heavy-based saucepan. Peel potatoes and cut into medium-size pieces, add to saucepan, along with the remaining chopped ingredients. Simmer slowly for 45 minutes. Remove from stove and strip meat from bones before returning meat to saucepan and allowing it to cool.

This quantity is sufficient for two meals, unless you own a large dog. The fat that is present in this dish is very good for your dog, so it is important that you do not trim the meat.

CAPRICORN

The zodiacal sign of Capricorn commences on 21 December, but does not come into its full power until on or about 28 December.

Deep within the hidden recesses of the Capricorn dog's mind are nurtured secret hopes and dreams, which if given time are usually brought to fruition. A quiet determination strengthened by the desire to achieve usually ensures that he reaches the position of 'top dog', not only in his household but in the neighbourhood as well. Excellent manners and an air of superiority guarantee that the pet's social aspirations are fulfilled. Subsequently, the ability to retain poise in rowdy, uncontrolled situations earns respect and praise from others. An innate politeness reinforces this exceptional self-control, though at times the animal might convey an impression of timidity. In actual fact he chooses to wait quietly on the sidelines rather than rush into the fray, secure in the knowledge that his eventual bid for leadership will be recognised.

Because a Capricorn dog can normally be trusted to behave impeccably on social occasions, he is an ideal companion to include when on family outings or excursions of a similar nature, and it is unusual to have to call him to heel.

Without appearing to make a fuss, your pet soon establishes that he expects to have every need pandered to. Nevertheless, the Capricorn canine is careful not to be caught taking too many liberties with the comforts available to him, and has enough sense to heed authority by working more slowly towards his personal goals, should indiscretions be discovered.

Even the lowliest-born Capricorn dog is able to transmit an air of gentility and good breeding. He is careful to avoid invading the privacy of others, and a respect for personal belongings is deeply ingrained; rarely would you find him jumping on a bed with muddy paws. It seems he knows only too well that any impetuous actions will be repented at leisure, lessening his chances of being socially acceptable wherever he goes.

Raised voices fail to impress the Capricorn dog, but only strengthen his basic determination to avoid the stress that might result if he were involved in family arguments. As I have already mentioned, he is loath to interfere in the business of others, and intuition usually warns him to keep his opinions to himself.

The Capricorn pet is apt to be serious by nature, and his sense of duty is also highly developed, so it is unlikely he will want to move any great distance from his front gate. He chooses to seek a clearly defined path that offers security at the other end, and in this your canine may appear to lack imagination, preferring to adhere as much as possible to a fairly static routine. His even temperament contains a warm humour which is usually reserved for special occasions. The Capricorn dog is inclined to be introverted, rarely allowing excessive emotion to surface; conversely, he is easily embarrassed by spontaneous displays of affection. It may be that secretly your canine desires more attention than he is already receiving, but shyness prevents him from seeking it. A loving heart is sometimes hidden behind a facade of indifference.

Authority, if not used to change the habits of the Capricorn, is necessary to his well-being. It serves to define the boundaries for correct behaviour, apart from showing the animal his position in the household. Beware of taking advantage of your pet's strong sense of responsibility. If expectations are too high he may get discouraged. As already noted, this pet is sometimes seen as a pessimist, certainly there are occasions when he needs to generate a more positive attitude if he is to succeed in reaching desired goals.

Though more often than not an indoor dog, Capricorn needs to spend a lot of time partaking of the fresh air, especially as his skin is apt to be highly sensitive; denying him sunlight will increase the likelihood of excessive scratching occurring. You may have to coax him to go outside, but misgivings are usually short-lived.

If the Capricorn canine becomes stressed at all, pressure may be put upon the kidneys and stomach, but in most cases, a tenacious regard for life improves the animal's powers of self-preservation. In fact he strengthens with age; even if he seems weak as a puppy, a strong instinct for survival normally protects him from serious ailments, though joints are prone to arthritis with increasing age.

This pet is often exceptionally strong in the legs and feet, and like the goat, he has little fear of heights. He appears to climb over difficult obstacles with sure-footed ease, showing scant regard for slippery surfaces. Once the dog has made a decision as to where to plant his feet, there is nothing hesitant in his choice, because he rarely acts on impulse.

Although the animal has a preference for his own company, he looks forward to short periods of relaxation with other dogs. Older companions are found to be more interesting, having the wisdom of age so respected by Capricorn.

The most suitable colours to enhance his position in the household are all tones of grey, violet and purple — even black can be complementary. Genuine friendships are found with those born under Taurus, Virgo and Cancer.

*needs to spend a lot of time partaking of the fresh air . . .
has little fear of heights*

Hunter's Hot Pot

Very few Capricorn dogs will turn away from Hunter's Hot Pot, and its popularity is unlikely to wane, even if it is served regularly. As the Capricorn canine tends to have a sensitive skin, the egg and milk can be added at your discretion. Usually the pet born during this sign excels in social situations, and mealtimes are no exception, especially if others are present. Though definite in his tastes, and never hesitant in refusing something he considers unpalatable, the Capricorn dog gets more enjoyment from his food if it is served at the same time each day.

The amount of dried dog food you use depends on the size of the dog, but do buy a good brand and be guided by the manufacturer's instructions.

dried dog food, preferably chicken-flavoured
½ cup cooked rice
1 egg

1 tablespoon polyunsaturated oil
milk (optional)
½ cup grated carrot

Put dried food in a basin and just cover with boiling water. When the water has been absorbed, stir cooked rice into mixture. Add unbeaten egg and oil, stir again, and when slightly cooled fold in grated carrot. If the concoction appears dry, it may be moistened further by the addition of milk. A garnish of parsley gives a touch of colour to a rather bland dish.

THE WATER BEARER

AQUARIUS

The zodiacal sign of Aquarius commences on 21 January, but does not come into full power until on or about 28 January.

The dog born during this sign usually possesses an impersonal nature, preferring to observe her world objectively, without becoming emotionally involved in private issues. The Aquarian pet often tends to hide an isolation of spirit by seeking as many friendships as possible. These attachments are rarely valued for their content, but seen as transient encounters, leaving the dog free to continue along her own path of discovery.

There are times when the canine needs to be left completely alone, as frequent contact with others tends to leave her feeling moody and morose. On these occasions your Aquarian does enjoy her own company, so there is no reason to feel sorry for her, as she is usually occupied with solitary thoughts. Part of this dog lives in the future, her dreams transcend time and space. Much of the day is spent in reverie, journeying beyond the barriers of the mind to try and find tomorrow.

Usually the owner of an Aquarian is well aware of the pet's ability to understand an exceptional number of words. No doubt you have often been charmed by the sight of your dog cocking her head to one side when spoken to, or whining in obvious response to a question put to her. This certainly proves she has been blessed with intelligence and intuition.

her dreams transcend time and space . . . a quiet power
within the eyes

Paradoxically the Aquarian is often forgetful; whether it is deliberate or beyond her control, I cannot truthfully answer. Certainly it is time-consuming when you have to help her look for a ball or favourite toy that has been carefully hidden, and the whereabouts consequently forgotten. This animal allows her mind to float with the breeze, preferring to be free of all responsibility; therefore concentration is sometimes minimal.

The Aquarian dog has a tendency to be highly strung, so it is better to approach her quietly, and advise your visitors to do the same. Loud voices cause her to sometimes shake all over in a nervous tremor, especially if the tone is argumentative or aggressive. Though she may appear intrigued by the presence of newcomers in the household, she prefers to view them from a distance, to remain impersonal and coolly detached. A trusting nature is difficult for the Aquarian to acquire unless a lot of time is spent obtaining her confidence. When this has been achieved, your canine should develop a more mature attitude to the people about her, along with the poise necessary for withstanding awkward encounters.

The Aquarian pet respects good manners, so is normally exceptionally polite in her own environment. She is unlikely to be found begging at the table for titbits, or acting in an obsequious fashion when food is served. More often than not she will retreat under the table so as to allow the conversation to waft over her.

Though usually a quiet, well-behaved dog, the Aquarian occasionally likes to shock others by outbursts of rebellious behaviour. Maybe she has already dug up a large portion of the garden to find a suitable spot for her bone, or is piqued by the sight of seedlings standing neatly in freshly tilled soil. Whatever the offence, the animal suffers momentary pangs of guilt, as she is basically very honest in nature, and does regret untoward conduct.

There is a quiet power within the eyes of your dog, therefore she puts it to good use by subduing other canines who might wish to disturb her peace. It is against the Aquarian's principles to fight for a cause, but not because she is a coward; on the contrary; with a preference for going her own way in life, she has little time for arguments. If by any chance the animal has no choice but to defend herself, her immediate reaction is to strike out at an aggressor in a confused and haphazard way.

This pet is full of surprises, with many facets to her personality, some being contrary to others. Jealousy is rarely displayed, though, as her solitary status and analytical mind leave little room in her heart for envy. The Aquarian has the ability to create a mood of independence wherever she goes, loneliness sometimes flows around her, permeating the household. Her inner nervous tension is usually responsible for erratic behaviour, even when trying to sleep she finds it hard to settle without being restless for a while.

The dog born during this sign could have trouble with her circulatory system or suffer accidents to the teeth, but more often than not stomach problems arise if her nerves are not kept in check. Your pet prefers small amounts of food, meted out at different times during the day, rather than consuming it all at once. This method lessens the chances of upsetting her digestive system, besides, the Aquarian dog can be a very fastidious eater.

Children manage to make friends with this canine more easily than adults do. Providing they do not rush her or make sudden movements, she will accept them fairly readily, often with an unexpected burst of affection. The Aquarian loves to be loved, provided little is expected of her in return. She is usually a graceful animal, with a certain style and individuality that defies classification.

As she travels down life's highways the most suitable friendships are formed with Gemini, Libra, Scorpio and some Sagittarius canines. The trip might be made easier if she were surrounded by colours that are favourable for Aquarians, namely electric blues and greys.

Hound Dog's Hash

As she races through the fields of her dreams in pursuit of an undefinable quarry, the Aquarian dog is a solitary and sometimes lonely animal. I mention this, because even when she is eating, other projects will sometimes take her mind away from food. Hound Dog's Hash can be relied upon to hold the interest of the Water Bearer, and have her asking for more. With its clever combination of ingredients, most pets would deem it a palate-pleaser. To strengthen her teeth, offer her a large meaty bone an hour or so after dinner.

minced lamb	*1 egg*
polyunsaturated oil	*parsley*
3 potatoes (mashed)	*milk*

Add oil to minced lamb and shape into a loaf. Place on a greased baking dish in a moderate oven. Cook for 20 minutes before removing from oven. Make sure mashed potato is of a good consistency (the addition of a little milk should help). Spread over loaf as evenly as possible, before making a well in the top. Add one egg and return to the oven for five minutes. I can highly recommend this dish for a special occasion, for it lends itself well when celebrations are at hand. As a final touch, decorate with a sprig of parsley.

Finally, I would like to add that the recipe is worthy of a more inspiring name, but it has been known as Hound Dog's Hash for many generations and tradition demands that it remains so.

P

THE FISH

PISCES

The zodiacal sign of Pisces commences on 20 February, but does not come into its full power until about 27 February.

The dog born under the sign of Pisces is sure to possess a natural understanding of life from the moment he opens his eyes and perceives the world around him. You will be beguiled by his charming manner, and sometimes irritated by his bouts of pessimism, but this dog is never a boring companion. He can show an occasional outburst of temper, and has attacks of melancholia, but these do not last; he can easily be won over with kind words and sympathetic treatment.

The Pisces dog is a mystical creature, having an air of delicate vulnerability about his person. He appears to soak up all the vibrations around him, but this tendency to absorb the colour and mood of his environment can dull his senses.

The Pisces pet has a dual element in his nature, and like the fish he represents, is able to surface very quickly, so if life is good stays at the top. In his darkest hours he will dive to the bottom and retreat into a world filled with blackness and despair. On these occasions he is inclined to brood, imagining the whole household is against him. He has the strength of character, though, to throw off such moods, and until another bout of melancholia overtakes him faces life with a sunny expression on his face.

Because of the Pisces dog's affinity with water, the owner will find him at his best in this element. Taking him for a walk along the beach, or near stretches of water, will do marvels for his constitution and mental well-being. He prefers a bright, sunny and preferably dry climate, and needs a lot of exercise, but sometimes has to be coerced to set foot outside, especially if the weather is inclement.

This dog loves to travel, and being constantly on the move suits his personality well; notice how he leaps into the family car at the slightest hint of an outing. The Pisces pet dislikes being contained for too long in one place, and if kept against his will in a confined area shows his displeasure by causing damage to property. When the reality of life becomes rather difficult to face, he escapes into a world of fantasy, where he can dream away the hours, a contented expression playing about his features.

Some Pisces dogs are very self-indulgent, and too easy-going. As this dog prefers to swim with the tide, he can easily be influenced by false friends, thus forming undesirable associations. By nature he is timid, fearful of cats and strange people amongst other things. He is also likely to turn tail and run, rather than assess the situation in a logical manner.

The Pisces canine has a lot of humour and gentle compassion in his soul, providing he has an owner who can assist in bringing out all the best aspects of his personality. This is no easy task to perform, as few manage to follow his quicksilver changes.

Life is a huge stage for this animal; and he is inclined to observe it as if through the eyes of a fish, elusive and fleeting with the shimmering, effervescent quality of water. The Fish is the twelfth sign of the zodiac, so the Pisces dog tends to be a representation of all that has gone before, a symbol also of death and eternity. Therefore, the nature of Pisces is a blend of all twelve signs; the knowledge of the past clutters his mind with conflicting thoughts.

The air of a mystic hangs about your pet, and it is possible he has experienced many lives, retaining the wisdom and

This dog loves to travel

memory of each. He certainly is of the belief that he can live forever — watch him cavort and strut upon his stage. In actual fact, his inability to look after his health correctly usually shortens his life span drastically. The dog needs extra vitamins to see him through his day, and warm comfortable sleeping quarters. He is better if he can conserve his energy as much as possible, because he does not have a great deal of this to spare. He tends to dart from place to place, and accepts every dog in the neighbourhood as a friend; it is rare to find him acting in an aggressive manner towards his peers. He is more inclined to be in the centre of a group of new friends, accepted without question.

A Pisces dog can be very weak as a puppy, so is seldom strong in adulthood. He has a slow metabolism, sometimes being indifferent to food and oblivious to his surroundings when a black mood is upon him. He is apt to suffer from foot trouble, and sometimes has difficulty in walking as he grows older. He is also prone to disorders of the blood, poor circulation and anaemia.

Being highly emotional creates health problems also; but good health can be maintained by using basic common sense. The owner should supervise the animal's diet and other activities as much as possible.

The Pisces dog often appears to be unable to understand his own personality, though he sees others very clearly, and it is unlikely he wll be easily fooled, except when he has to come to grips with himself.

This pet finds his most lasting friendships with others in his own sign, or with those born under Gemini, Virgo and Scorpio. He is soothed by all shades of mauve, violet and purple, as these are colours that stabilise a Pisces mood.

Once you have fathomed some of the complexities of the Piscean nature, you will have a rapport with your dog that others will envy.

Fantasy Fish Flan

With the fish as his symbol I felt it would be appropriate to bring a taste of the sea to the Pisces dog. The following recipe is best kept for a special occasion, especially if you are already trying to stretch the family budget.

The Pisces pet benefits from the unexpected, and not only will this dish be a surprise, it should direct his dreams towards the wide expanses of water he loves so much. The addition of meat helps sustain a sense of normality that would otherwise not be there, and is a reminder of basic fare, which is never far away. Pisces also loves to party, and this meal is most suitable for sharing with canine friends.

1 whole fish	*1 dessertspoonful olive oil*
1 egg	*¾ cup milk*
mincemeat	*breadcrumbs*

Combine the mincemeat with the oil, and line a pie dish with this mixture. Flake the raw fish (without bones) over the top of the meat before adding the lightly beaten egg and milk. Sprinkle with breadcrumbs and bake in a moderate oven for approximately ½ hour, or until the custard sets.